Play Banjo Today!

A Complete Guide to the Basics

by Colin O'Brien

Recording Credits:
Colin O'Brien, Banjo, Guitar & Narration
Recorded at Buckaroo Studios,
Milwaukee, WI

ISBN 978-1-4234-6642-0

HAL•LEONARD®
CORPORATION

7777 W. BLUEMOUND RD. P.O. BOX 13819 MILWAUKEE, WI 53213

In Australia Contact:
Hal Leonard Australia Pty. Ltd.
4 Lentara Court
Cheltenham, Victoria, 3192 Australia
Email: ausadmin@halleonard.com.au

Visit Hal Leonard Online at
www.halleonard.com

Introduction

Track 1

Welcome to *Play Banjo Today! Level 2*. This book is for players already familiar with bluegrass basics. The material presented will include advanced bluegrass (an extension of *Play Banjo Today! Level 1*) as well as melodic style, single-string style, and chord melody. Music theory is presented, applied, and integrated into the lessons throughout the book. The written music in this book is a bridge—it leads you to where the music is. When you fully know a piece, you no longer need to read the music—it is memorized in your mind and your fingers.

The "strike zone" is where a good baseball pitcher throws the ball, and it's also where a banjoist keeps their fingers. It is important to keep the left- and right-hand fingers in the strike zone (close to the strings at all times). The left-hand fingers should stay within about an inch of the strings when they're not fretting notes. If they stray farther away (for instance, the pinky tends to straighten out), it just means they've got farther to travel to get back to the strings! You'll find it easier to execute clean, left-hand techniques (hammer-ons, pull-offs, slides, etc.) with confidence when playing within the strike zone. The strike zone also applies to the right hand; the fingers should always be within about an inch of the strings.

Another subject worthy of attention is the importance of playing steady rhythm. If you're playing with a relaxed, steady, groovy rhythm and you play a wrong note, it will probably be okay—it may even come out sounding like a lick! On the other hand, if you play all the right notes but are lacking a relaxed, rhythmic feel, it's simply not going to be enjoyable to play or listen to. Ultimately, it could be argued that it would be better to play the wrong note at just the right time than it would to play the right note at the wrong time. The **metronome** is a great tool to get the rhythm of your playing together. With every click, it tells you where the beat is in true mathematical time. The goal is not to play like a metronome, but rather cultivate a relaxed relationship with true time. As you become comfortable playing along with the metronome, you'll find it can infuse your practice sessions with a meditative quality. It is also a great tool for organizing your practice sessions. For instance, when you're working on your speed, the metronome tells you at what **tempo** (beats per minute) you are able to play a particular tune or passage. Write that number down, and that's the speed to exceed in your next session.

About the CD

All of the music written in this book is also on the CD. Each example on the CD has a corresponding track number next to the written music. Listening to the music on the CD is so important, it actually counts as practice! Music is not a visual art, and we need to hear it to fully internalize it.

About the Author

Author Colin O'Brien travels throughout the U.S.A. performing concerts and presenting workshops. His solo concerts feature banjo, fiddle, guitar, and his amazing foot percussion. He is also a member of the award-winning band Salt Creek. Colin is also the author of *Play Banjo Today! Level 1*. He'd love to hear from you at *www.colingobrien.com*.

Contents

Bluegrass

Bill Monroe, the father of bluegrass music, began playing professionally in the 1920s. At that time, the banjo was still regarded as a four-string rhythm instrument used in jazz ensembles. It wasn't until 1945, when Monroe gave Earl Scruggs a job, that the banjo became a featured instrument in country music. Monroe's new-sounding music combined the blues and Scotch-Irish influences (fiddle tunes) with an adventurous imagination. The sound of Monroe's group in 1945 came to define what we know of as bluegrass.

The four banjo **breaks** (solos) in this lesson use the bluegrass techniques presented in *Play Banjo Today! Level 1*: *forward roll, inside-outside roll, forward-reverse roll, pinches, slides, hammer-ons*, and *pull-offs*. These right- and left-hand techniques are freely woven into the arrangements to provide rhythmic interest and to bring out the melody.

Track 2

Playing the Words

"Goin' Down That Road Feelin' Bad," "Nine Pound Hammer," "Will the Circle Be Unbroken," and "Hand Me Down My Walkin' Cane" all are *songs*, which is to say they are sung. When the vocalist sings, they use words, pitch, rhythm, and inflection to express music. The arrangements presented here are instrumental breaks; they can be played as solos between the vocalists' singing. By playing with a steady rhythm and emphasizing the melody notes, you can play the words on your banjo! The lyrics of the following songs are written below their melody notes. These are the notes that should have most emphasis, the other notes being played quieter. The banjo now gets to sing the words with its own voice!

Recommended Listening: Earl Scruggs, John Hartford, Sonny Osborne, J.D. Crowe, and whomever these fine players listen to.

Hammer-On the C Chord

Below you'll see a C lick with a snazzy hammer-on. Once memorized (that shouldn't take long!), look at your left hand and make sure that your 2nd finger is hammering just behind the fret and that it never leaves the strike zone. Playing this is not about power, but relaxed accuracy.

Track 3

Hammer in the Sea

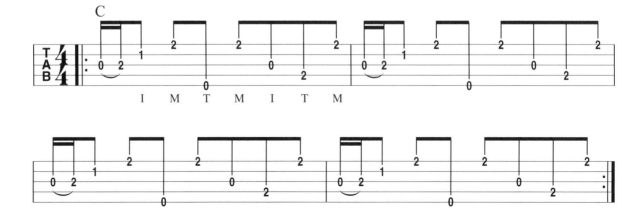

Goin' Down That Road Feelin' Bad

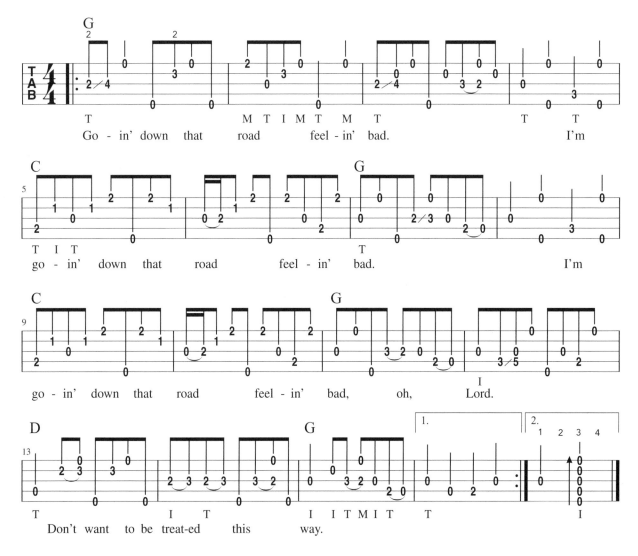

Check out this new pull-off lick. Be sure to keep the 1st finger of the left hand down between pull-offs. Try them two ways: pulling toward the floor or pushing toward the ceiling.

Track 5

New Pull-Off Lick

► Try these pull-offs in other songs you play as well.

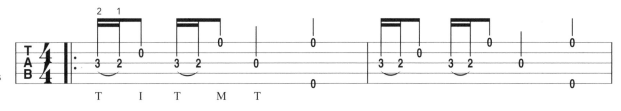

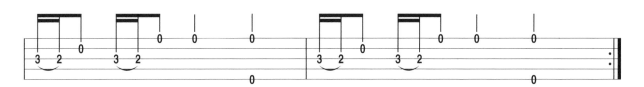

Will the Circle Be Unbroken

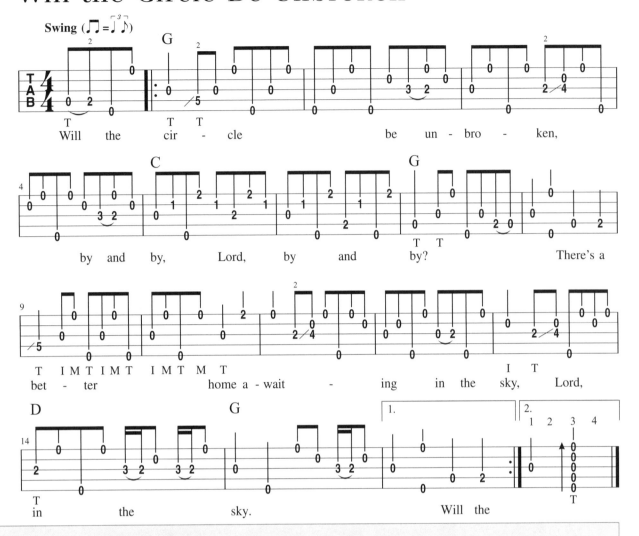

Swing Feel and Triplets

When you listen to "Will the Circle Be Unbroken" on the CD you'll be hearing what is called *swing feel*. Swing is a rhythmic feel that is easily heard, but difficult to notate. Other terms used to describe it are "shuffle feel," "dotted feel," or "lilt." Swing could also be described as delaying the upbeats in music. One measure of eighth notes is counted "1 & 2 & 3 & 4 &." The upbeats are the "ands." Play the upbeats a little late without budging the downbeats and you're exploring swing territory.

The next song, "Nine Pound Hammer," uses a new rhythm called a *triplet*. A triplet is three notes, as the name implies. In the next song a triplet appears in measure 7, and it takes up the same rhythmic space as one quarter note, or two eighth notes. A fun way to sing triplets is "sci ba da, di ba da, sci ba da, di ba da!" "Sci ba da" takes up one beat and "di ba da" also takes up one beat. Both triplets and swing underscore an important point: if you want to learn it, listen to it!

Track 7

Before playing "Nine Pound Hammer," try these hammer-ons and pull-offs on for size. The eighth-note part of this lick (first two beats of each measure) can be used as an alternate lick in some other songs you already know—it fits well in many places!

Pull-Off/Hammer-On Combo

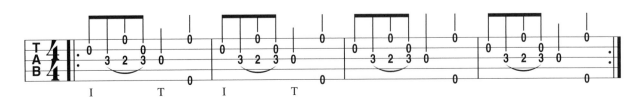

Nine Pound Hammer

Track 8

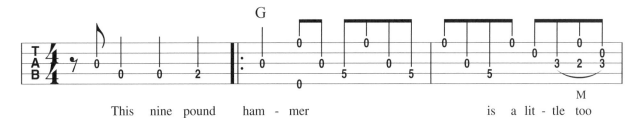

This nine pound ham - mer is a lit - tle too

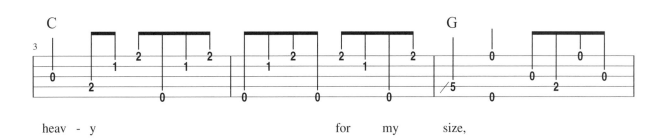

heav - y for my size,

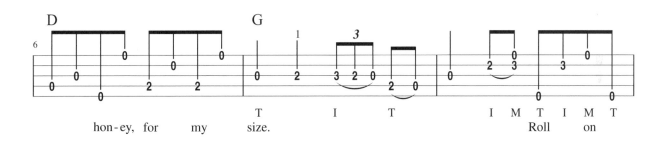

hon-ey, for my size. Roll on

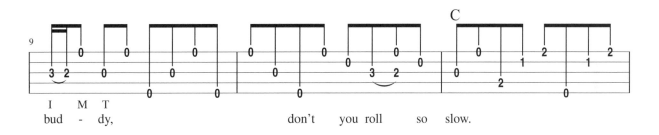

bud - dy, don't you roll so slow.

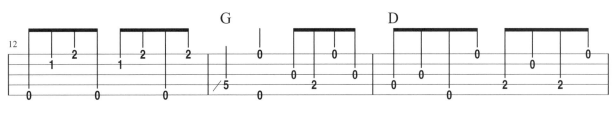

Tell me, how can I pull when the wheels won't

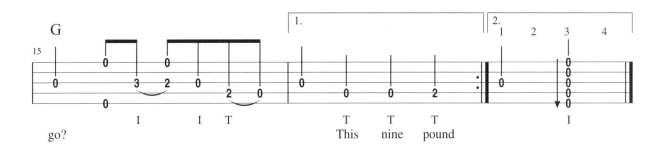

go? This nine pound

7

The lead-in here lick here is very similar to the one used in "Will the Circle Be Unbroken."

Hand Me Down My Walkin' Cane

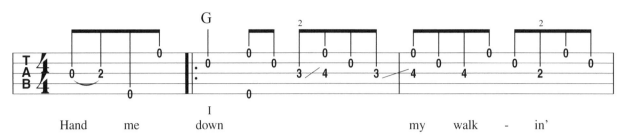

Hand   me   down   my   walk - in'

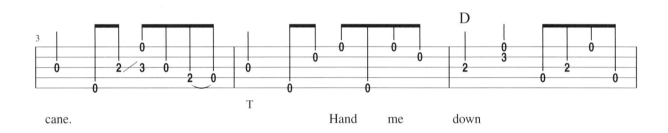

cane.   Hand   me   down

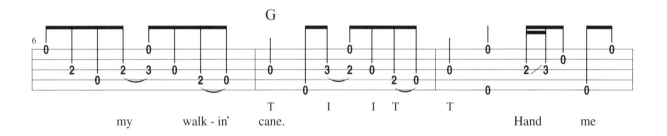

my   walk - in'   cane.   Hand   me

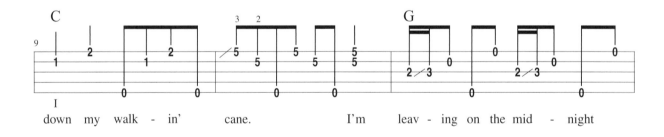

down   my   walk - in'   cane.   I'm   leav - ing on the mid - night

► In measure 11, you'll find a lick right out of "Cripple Creek" from *Play Banjo Today! Level 1* (and many other places).

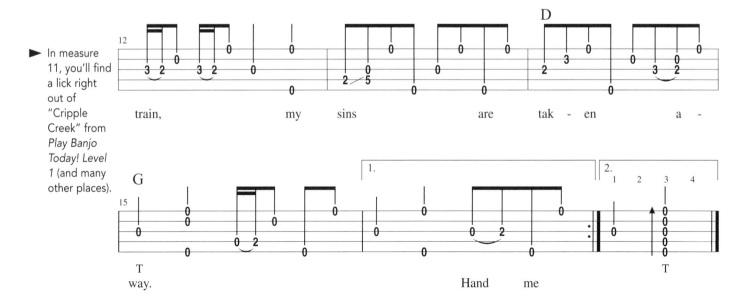

train,   my   sins   are   tak - en   a -

way.   Hand   me

Bending

Track 10

Bending from, Bending to

There are three components to a *bend*: where it starts, where it ends, and what happens in between (the bending note itself). First, make sure you establish the note you're bending from. That is, let the unbent note sound (perhaps for just an instant) and then bend it. When you bend a note, you raise its pitch. The notation shows a curved arrow pointing toward the step value, such as 1/2 (a half step). Here's how that sounds.

Track 11

Bend Exercise

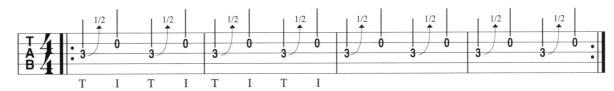

The Flat 3rd or "Blue Note"

If you play the 4th fret of the G string without bending the note you're playing the note B. This is the third note of a G major scale (G–A–**B** or DO–RE–**MI**) and is called a *major 3rd*. Now move the note to the 3rd fret of the G string. This note is B♭ (B flat). You have *flatted* (lowered) the third note of the scale, so it's now called a *flat third* (or *minor 3rd*). This is a highly expressive note! The above Bend Exercise is a good example of the flat 3rd resolving to a major 3rd. In general, flat (minor) 3rds imply tension and major 3rds have a resolved, happy sound. By bending the B♭ (flat 3rd) up toward the B (as in the above exercise), you hear its bluesy, expressive effect. Be sure to listen to the CD!

Track 12

► This song is in the key of F. The chord progression is common in jazz and is known as a VI-II-V-I progression.

Don't Let Your Deal Go Down

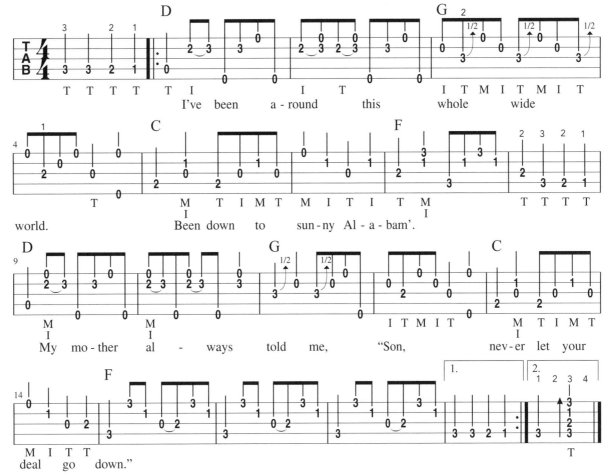

Track 13

Here's how the flat 3rd bend sounds an octave higher up the neck.

High-Bend Exercise

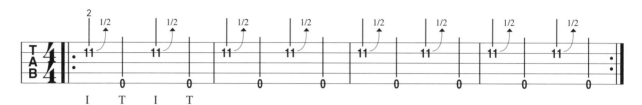

Partial Chord Shapes

Several pieces in this book use *partial chord shapes*. Each shape uses notes from F, D, or A closed-position chord shapes. However, only the notes played are held down with the left hand, hence the name "partial chord shape." It's a good idea to visualize and understand what F, D, or A chord each of the partial chord shapes correspond with. This will help make visible the logic of the fretboard. Knowing *why* you put your fingers down helps you remember *where* you put them.

Partial Chord Tutorial

Here's the key used throughout this book for partial chords:

○ = unused notes in chord
◯ = notes held down

The following partial chord shapes are used in "Goin' Down That Road Feelin' Bad."

The G chord uses part of the A barre shape:

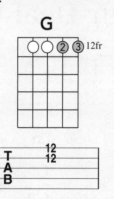

The C and D chords each use part of the F shape:

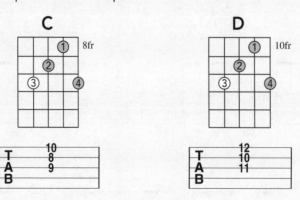

The following high break arrangement of "Goin' Down That Road Feelin' Bad" uses partial chord shapes. It'd be a good idea to play backup along with the CD using the full chords in all three chord zones (from *Play Banjo Today! Level 1*).

Goin' Down That Road Feelin' Bad
(High Break)

▶ Play backup using the full chord shapes and visualize the partial chords within them. The more points of familiarity you perceive, the easier it will be to navigate the neck with confidence.

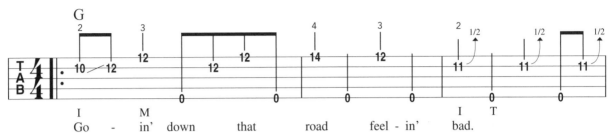

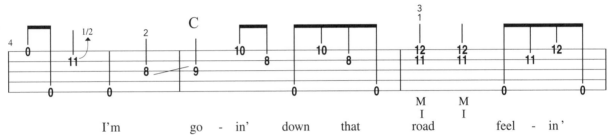

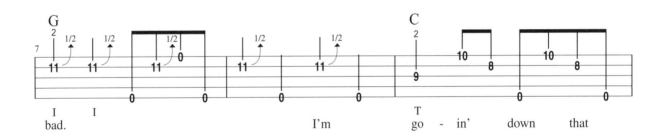

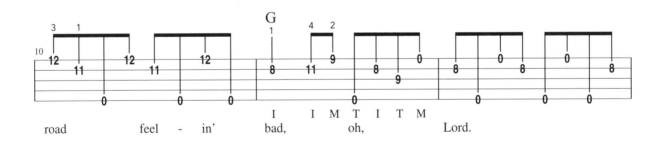

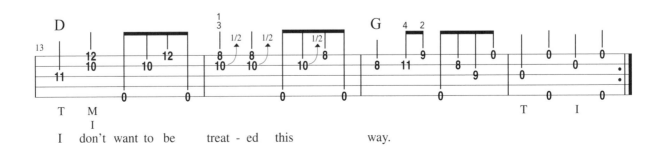

11

Melodic Style

The *melodic style* differs from bluegrass in both execution and sound. As a general rule, every note is played on a different string—some open, some fretted. This results in a smooth, melodious sound from the banjo. The melodic style is much less dependent on right-hand picking patterns than bluegrass. The left hand makes ample use of partial chord shapes and alterations thereof. It's not unusual for every note in a melodic arrangement to be a melody note (another big difference from bluegrass). Banjoist Bill Keith developed this technique as a way of tackling fiddle tunes on the banjo.

The three G scale positions here apply directly to the following tunes: "Turkey in the Straw," "The Flowers of Edinburgh," "The Road to Lisdoonvarna," "Planxty Irwin," "The Kesh Jig," "The Irish Washerwoman," "Blackberry Blossom," and "Mason's Apron."

G Major Scale: Three Ways to Play It

Basic:

► Be sure to keep the left-hand fingers on their notes until after you play the next note. This will dovetail the ringing notes into each other for a smooth, flowing sound.

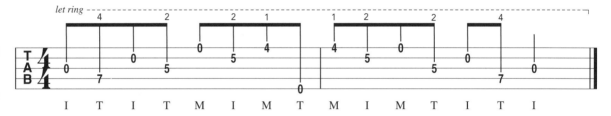

This one involves wrapping the fret-hand thumb around the neck to fret the 5th string.

Extended:

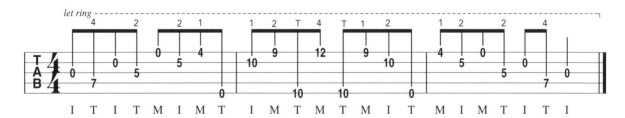

Here's a New Way Up:

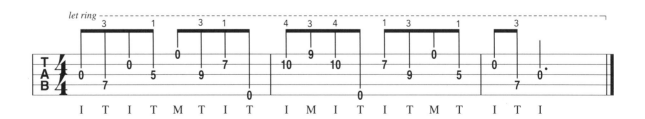

Recommended Listening: Tony Trischka, Bill Keith, and Béla Fleck's *Fiddle Tunes for Banjo* (Rounder #3719).

Lesson 4 | Reels

Track 19

Let's keep it reel folks. A *reel* is both a tune and a type of folk dance. Common in Scotland and Ireland, the reel is characterized by its rhythm, which accents the first and third beats of each measure. Reels usually have two *sections* (A and B); in most reels, each section is repeated (to create an AABB form). The melody often follows a scheme of a two-measure question and a two-measure answer phrase. Did I mention they sound wonderful on the banjo?

Two New Partial Chords

"Turkey in the Straw" uses two new partial chords to add to your expanding library.

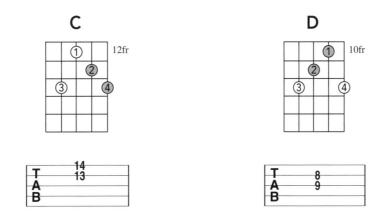

Music History

"Turkey in the Straw" is a well-known American folk song from the early 19th century. It was first popularized in the 1820s and '30s. Though not directly Scotch-Irish in origin, it does fit into the category of reels. It's also a popular ice cream truck melody! What's better than a banjo? A banjo *and* ice cream.

Following the Roadmap

You may notice some new roadmap directions in the next song. *D.S. al Coda* means to go to the sign (𝄋), play to the measure with the *To Coda* sign, then jump directly to the *Coda* section.

Turkey in the Straw

► "Turkey in the Straw" also uses a third partial chord you've already learned; can you find it?

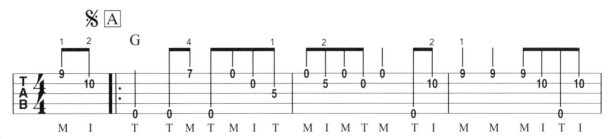

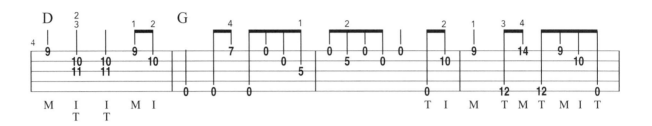

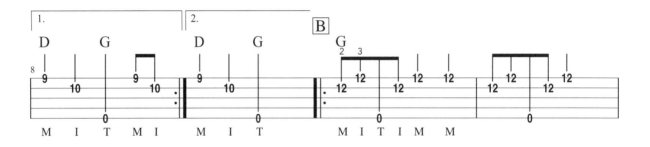

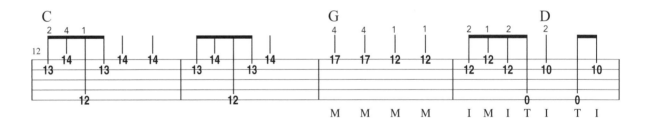

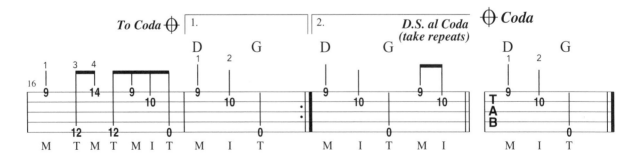

Backing Up

When playing backup, your primary purpose is to support the lead singer or instrument. This means providing a good rhythm and harmonic support by emphasizing chord tones. One must be careful, however, to not interfere with the melody.

Following the Roadmap

A new roadmap direction appears in the next song: **D.C.** This means go to the top of the form and play all the way through the song again.

Track 22

Turkey in the Straw
(Backup)

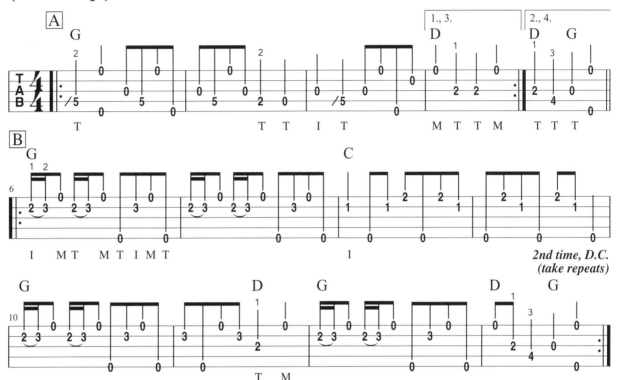

Track 23

What's a Major Scale?

A *major scale* has seven different notes, with the "eighth" note being an octave higher than the first (as with the G scale you learned). The eight notes are arranged in a pattern of **whole steps** (the distance of two frets) and **half steps** (the distance of one fret). These two distances between notes are called **intervals**. The pattern of intervals for all major scales is W–W–H–W–W–W–H. Here's how that looks on the neck:

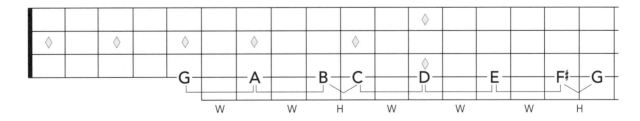

Here's the same thing in tab. Use the first finger of the left hand to play the following notes.

G Major Along One String

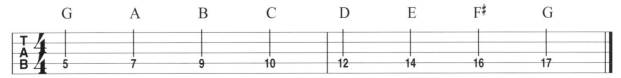

Change One Note

To play a D major scale, we need to change one note from the G scale. The first note of the D major scale is the note D. If you look at the notes of the G scale and read the intervals from D to D, you'll see that they are W–W–H–W–W–H–W. This is not the major scale pattern. We need our pattern back! To do this, we raise the last note by one half step and *poof!*

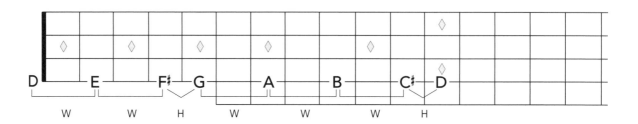

D Major Along One String

► Look at the letter names of the G and D scales and you'll see that they differ by just one note: C♯.

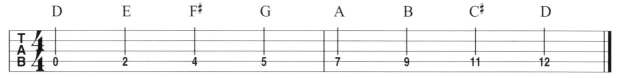

D Major: Three Ways to Play It

Track 24

Basic:

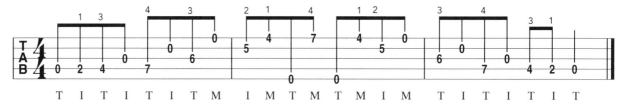

Track 25

Extended:

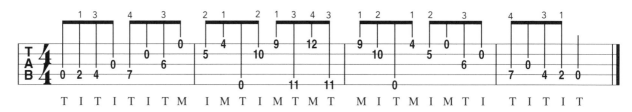

A New Way Up:

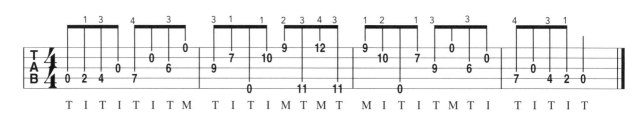

16

The Silver Spear

► Listen for the triplets that are played the second time through the tune, then check out the exercises that follow.

► In the last measure, "Harm." stands for *harmonic*. Simply lay your fingers over the 7th fret wire without pushing down and strum the strings for a chiming effect.

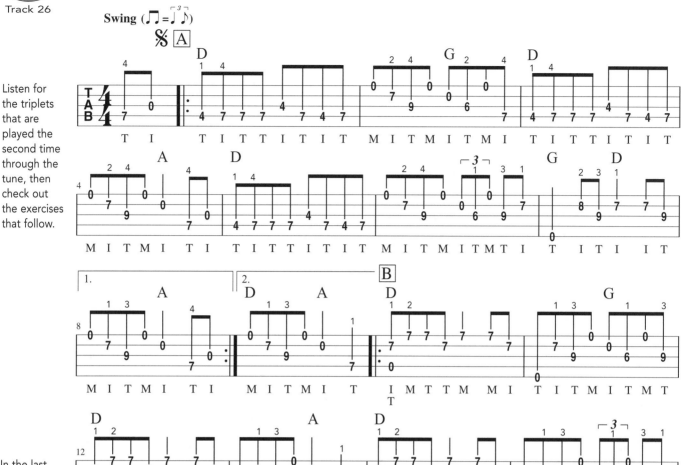

Triplets for the Silver Spear

The triplets replicate what you might hear played on the fiddle or bagpipes. The triplets below are played the second time through the tune on the CD. They occur in measures 1, 3, and 5. Enjoy 'em!

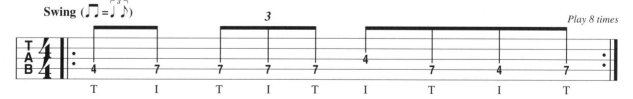

Here's a nice way to get the hang of triplets:

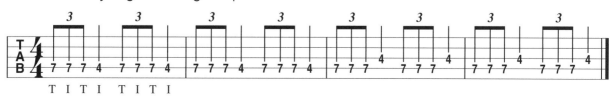

17

Track 29

So far everything in this book has been written in a 4/4 *time signature*. The top number of the 4/4 time signature indicates there are four beats in each measure of music. The bottom number indicates that a quarter note gets counted as one beat. (Each quarter note takes up one beat, so four quarter notes equal one measure.) Now let's change the numbers! Our next tune is in **6/8 time**. Each measure now has six beats (6), and each eighth note (8) is worth one beat. Six eighth notes equal one measure of 6/8 time.

Play these notes using the thumb and index fingers of the right hand:

Track 30

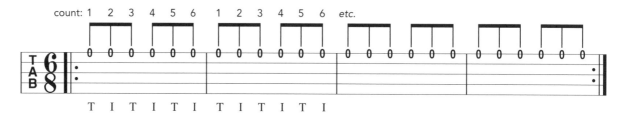

In any time signature, a quarter note is always twice as long as an eighth note. Remember that, in 6/8 time, an eighth note gets one beat, so in 6/8 time, quarter notes get counted as two beats. Fancy math indeed!

Track 31

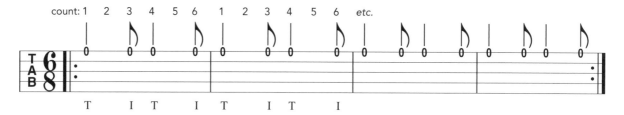

Track 32

Dotted Quarter Notes

When you see a **dot** after a note, you increase its value by 1/2. In 6/8 time, each eighth note gets one beat (remember that is what the bottom number of the time signature tells us), and each quarter note gets two beats. When there is dot after a quarter, we add half its value (one beat), so a dotted quarter receives three beats. Two of them fit into each six-beat measure.

Track 33

Track 34

Dotted Eighth Notes

In 6/8 time, we know each eighth note gets a beat. If we divide an eighth note in half, we have two sixteenth notes. When we dot a note, we increase its value by 1/2, so a dotted eighth is increased in duration by a sixteenth note. The dotted eighth takes up the time of three sixteenth notes. Each dotted eighth in the example below is followed by a sixteenth note, which receives a quick half beat. Be sure to listen to this rhythm on the CD to help it make more sense!

Track 35

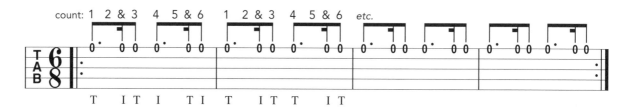

Planxty Irwin

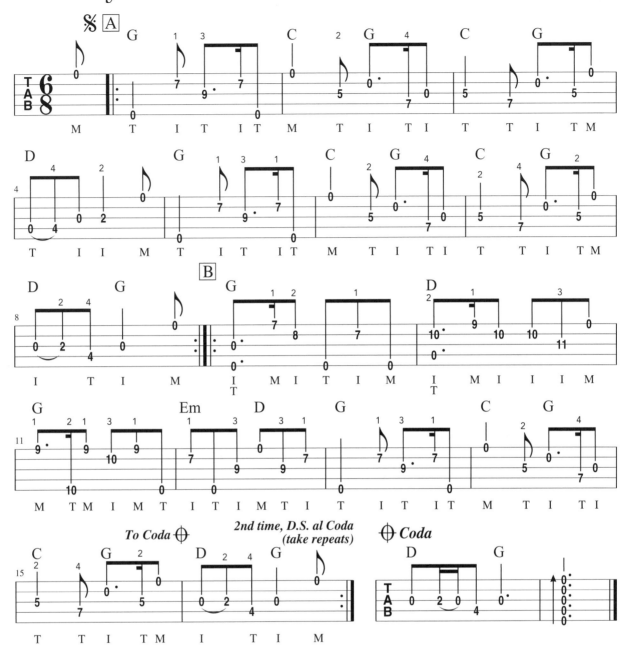

On the recording, you'll hear the last measure of the A and B section sometimes played like this:

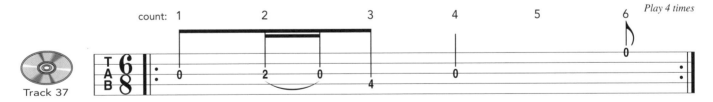

Music History

A *planxty* refers to a piece of music written as a tribute to a person, usually a patron of the composer. Traveling musicians wrote songs for others in return for beds, meals, or bills paid. In return, the patron was honored by their name being used as the title for the composition. "Planxty Irwin" was written by traveling Harper-composer Turlough O'Carolan (1670–1738) for Colonel John Irwin. A plaque in St. Patrick's Cathedral in Dublin honors O'Carolan as "the last of the Irish bards"—the man who brought to a close the centuries-old tradition of the wandering poet minstrel.

Going Modal

Modes are an ancient system of organizing musical tones common in medieval liturgical music. There are seven modes, each relating to a note of the major scale. You have already played the first mode: *Ionian* (also known as the "major scale")! The second mode is *Dorian*. You can play the Dorian mode by starting any major scale on its second note. Starting on the second note of the scale changes the order of half and whole steps, and that changes the scale's sound. Our next tune, "The Road to Lisdoonvarna" is in the Dorian mode. In this tune, we start the D major scale on its second note, E. This is called E Dorian.

E Dorian Along One String

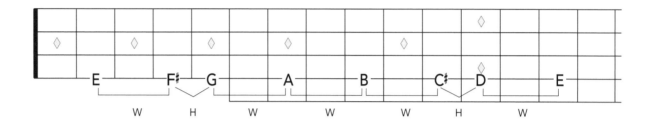

Play the scale below. Prime your ears by strumming E minor (measure 1). If you can make the stretch, use the 2nd finger where indicated to allow the notes to ring as much as possible. These sounds perhaps invoke the cool, foggy woods along the road to Lisdoonvarna.

Dipping into Dorian

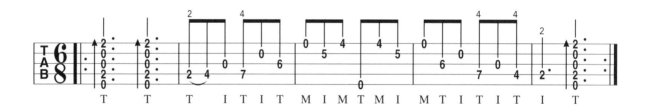

Music History

Plato felt that playing music in a certain mode would incline one towards specific feelings and behaviors associated with that mode. He suggested that soldiers listen to music in the Dorian mode to make them feel stronger. He also believed that a change in the musical modes of the state would cause a wide-scale social revolution.

This is a traditional Irish fiddle tune. Lisdoonvarna is a town in County Clare, Ireland.

The Road to Lisdoonvarna

▶ Whenever you see the note C♯ (a number 6 on the middle line), hold that note down as long as you can!

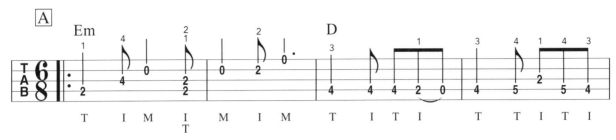

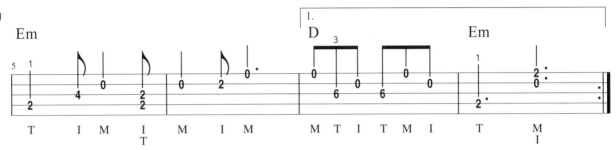

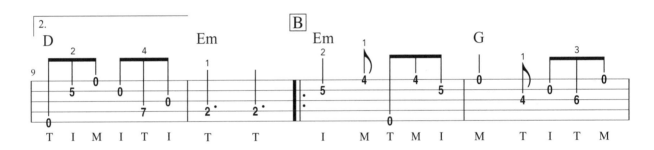

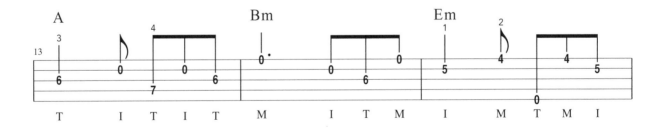

D.C.
(take repeats)

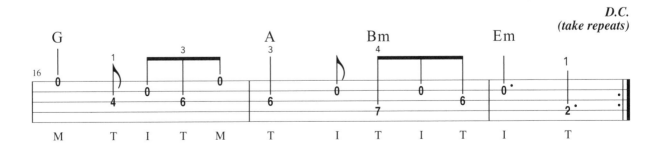

Track 41

The term *jig* refers both to a tune and the accompanying dance. Jigs are in 6/8 time. Before playing these roll patterns, listen to the CD. They are played with a rhythmic, "Irish lilt."

Three Rolls in 6/8 Time

The three following roll patterns will warm you up to the jig rhythm.

Track 42

The *forward-reverse roll* works well in 6/8 time:

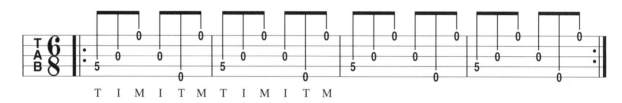

Track 43

Here's a variation:

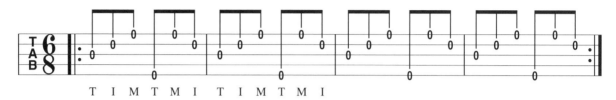

Track 44

One more:

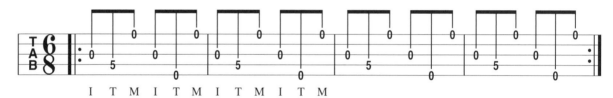

Music History

The term "jig" springs from two possible sources: the French word "Gigue," meaning "small fiddle," or the Italian word "*Giga*," which refers to a short piece of music popular in the Middle Ages. Irish jigs are short tunes commonly played on the fiddle.

Track 45

In measure 4 of "The Irish Washerwoman," there is a hammer-on of two notes at once. Play the example below to get the hang of it. The strings are not picked before you hammer on the notes. The sound produced has tone, but its primary function is rhythmic. The hammer-on provides a percussive sound to keep the jig rhythm dancing along. The 1st finger can stay down the whole time while the 2nd and 3rd fingers execute the hammer-ons. Be sure to give this a listen on the CD.

Track 46

Double Hammer-On

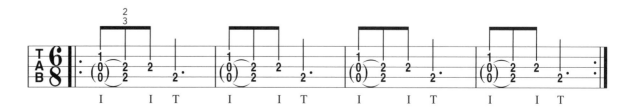

This tune is sometimes sung and played as a song.

The Irish Washerwoman

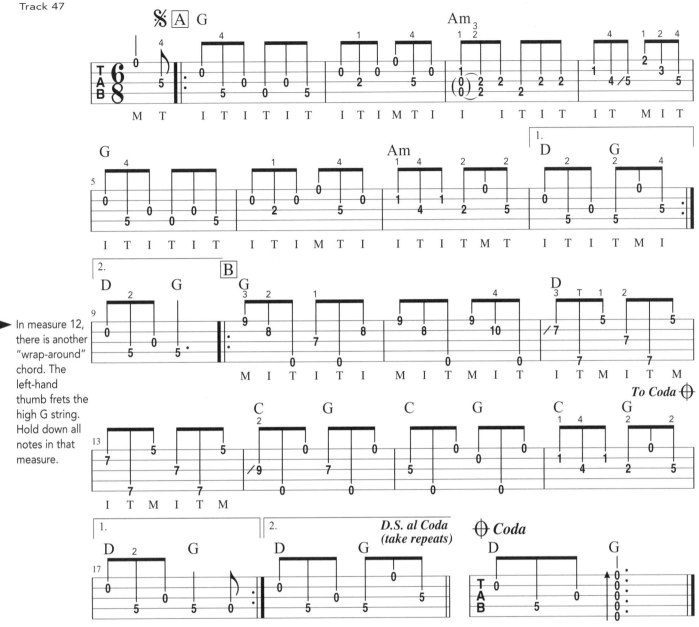

► In measure 12, there is another "wrap-around" chord. The left-hand thumb frets the high G string. Hold down all notes in that measure.

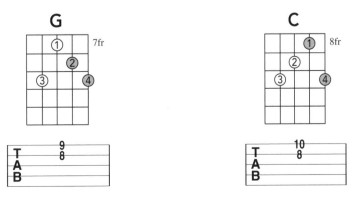

Recommended Listening: Irish fiddlers and bagpipers to enjoy and absorb the nuances of Irish music.

New Partial Chords

The B section of this backup arrangement makes use of the following partial chords:

The Irish Washerwoman
(Backup)

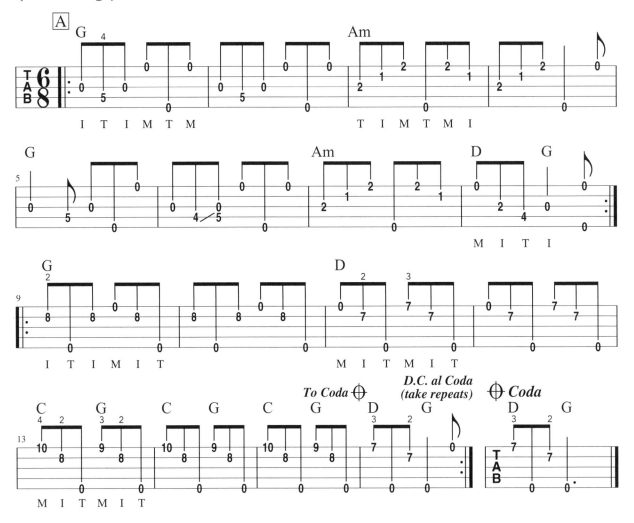

Kesh is a small village in County Fermanagh, Northern Ireland. It is situated on the Kesh River.

The Kesh Jig

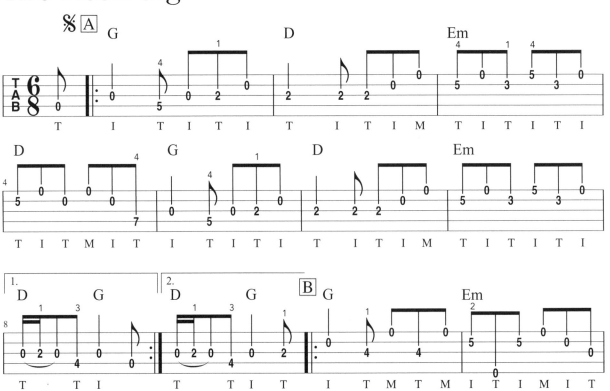

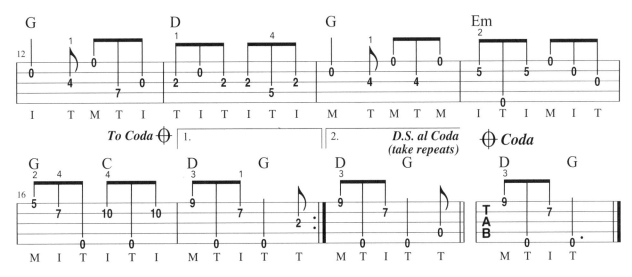

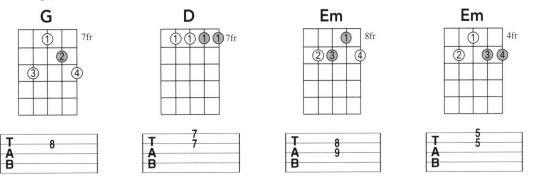

New Partial Chords

The following partial chords are used in the backup arrangement of "The Kesh Jig."

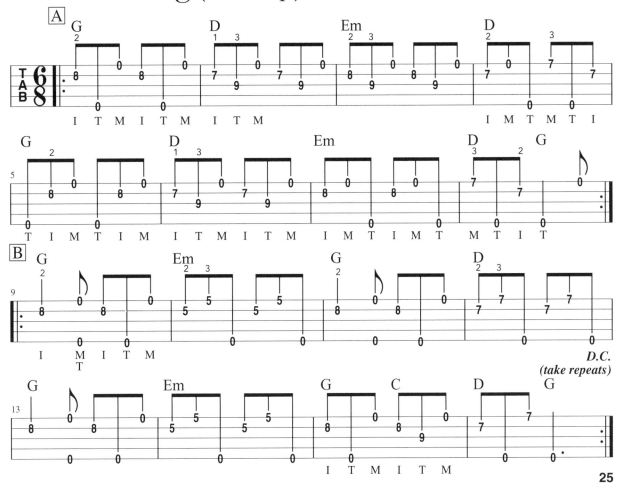

Now enjoy a melodious take on backup for "The Kesh Jig."

Track 50

The Kesh Jig (Backup)

Track 51

The *hornpipe* is a tune in 4/4 time similar to the reel. Unlike reels, however, hornpipes are played with a distinct, rhythmic lilt or swing, whereas reels are played "straight." This difference in rhythmic feel is notated with a "swing" icon above the music. Listen to the recording (and to Irish fiddle tunes) to absorb the rhythmic nuances as well.

Music History

The term "hornpipe" refers to both a dance **and** a musical style. One would dance the hornpipe to a hornpipe. Hornpipes have been played and danced since the 17th century. The hornpipe is also the name of an ancient wind instrument made from a cow horn that is sometimes converted into a bagpipe.

This tune is commonly played as a reel or played at light speed by bluegrass musicians. Here the tune is set as an easy-going hornpipe.

Track 52

Blackberry Blossom

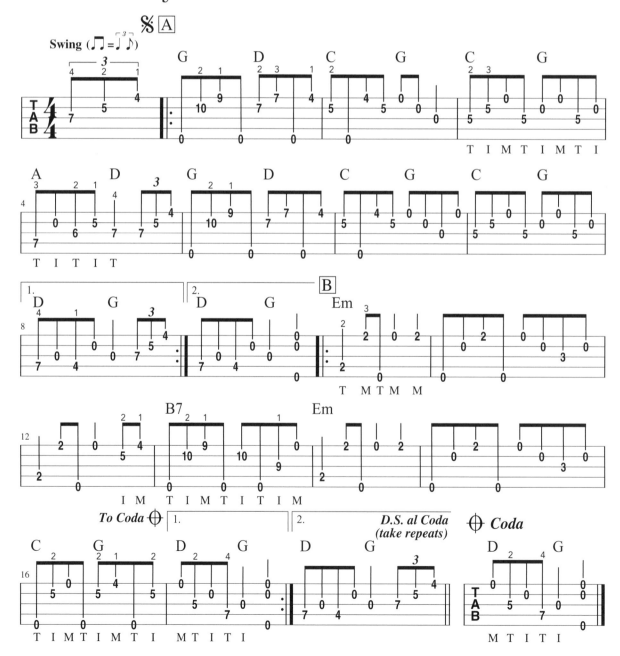

Blackberry Blossom (Backup)

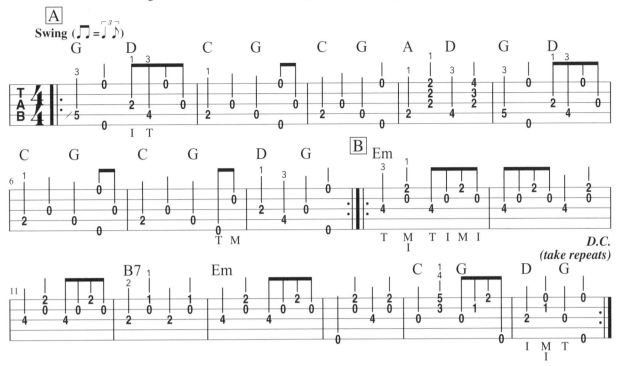

Edinburgh is the capital city of Scotland. Throughout the city are world-renowned parks and gardens.

Flowers of Edinburgh

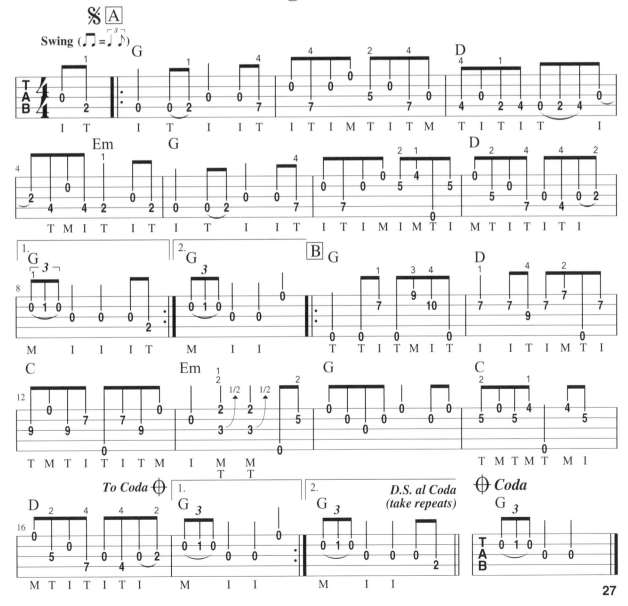

Lesson 9 | Polkas

Polkas are almost always written and played in *2/4 time* (two beats per measure).

Music History

The polka is a lively Central European dance and a genre of dance music familiar throughout Europe and the Americas. It originated in the mid-19th century in Bohemia and is still a common genre in Czech, German, Austrian, Slovakian, and Polish folk music. In Milwaukee, Wisconsin, the polka's still keepin' time!

The Irish band, Planxty, recorded this tune in 1979. They called it "John Ryan's Polka."

Sean Ryan's Polka

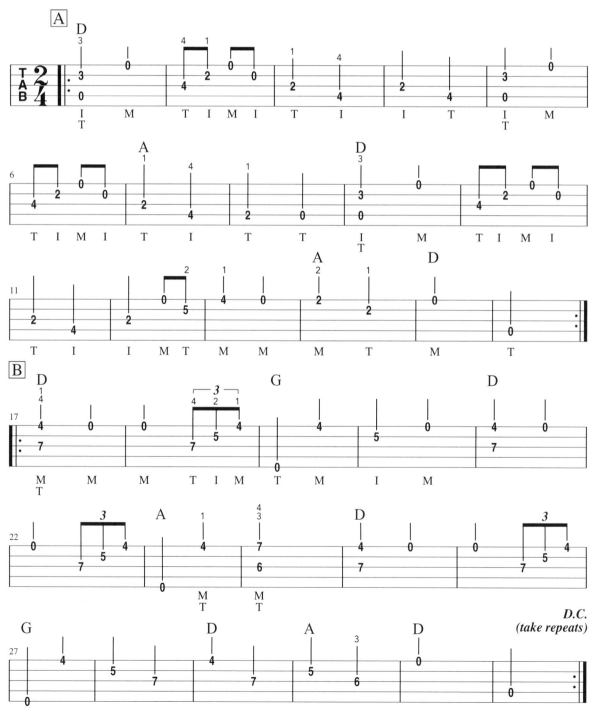

28

Sean Ryan's Polka
(High Break)

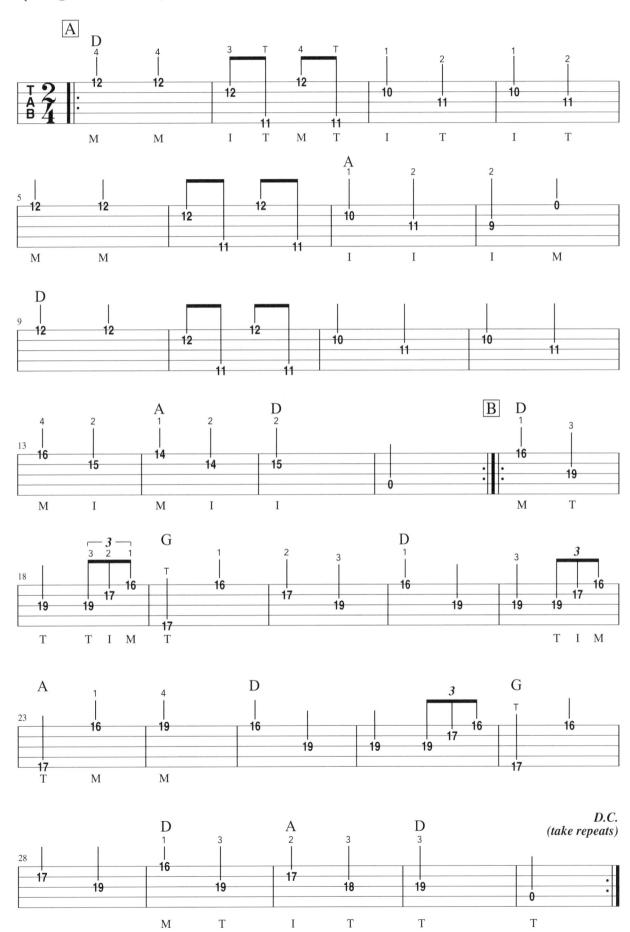

Single-String Style

Single-string style is where you play several notes in a row on the same string. The predominant right-hand fingering is T–I–T–I. This style first came to widespread attention thanks t o Don Reno. Béla Fleck incorporates the single-string style into his playing. Because there is usually only one note sounding at a time, the single-string style produces a punchy sound all its own.

Single-String Exercises

Play with a relaxed, even sound.

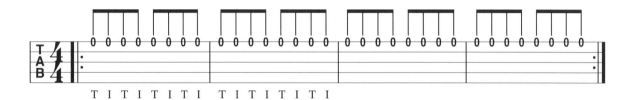

Play across four strings.

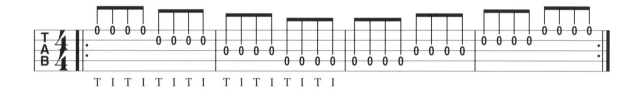

From low to high…

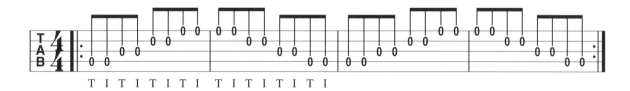

Leaving spaces…

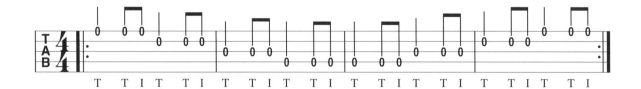

Crossing under...

Track 63

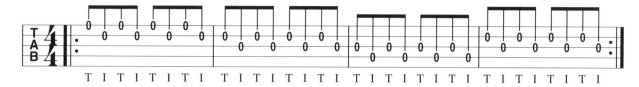

Name this tune!

Track 64

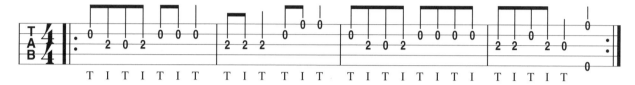

Recommended Listening: Don Reno and Béla Fleck. For a wide range of musical ideas that may work well with the single-string technique, listen to other instrumentalists (horn players, guitar players, etc.).

Track 65

Single-String Scales

The logic and linear nature of the single-string style makes it a wonderful way to visualize and learn scales. The G major scales below are both related to the F-shape G chord at fret 5.

Track 66

G Major #1

This scale plays straight through the F-shape G chord.

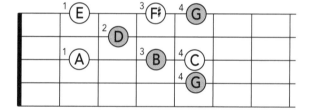

Here it is in tab.

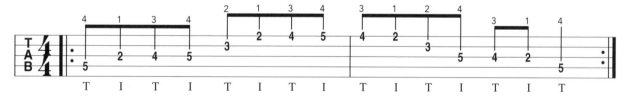

G Major #2

This G scale plays in front of the F-shape G chord.

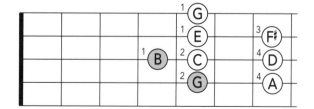

Here it is in tab.

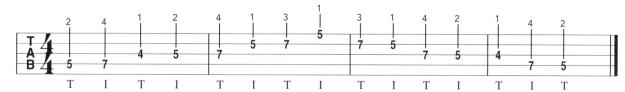

These are movable scales! Try them two frets higher and you're playing in A major. Here's one position that plays through the F shape in the key of A.

A Major

► Find the one played in front of the F shape on your own.

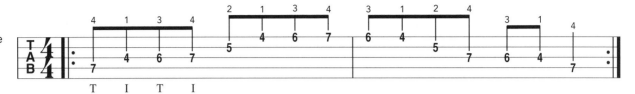

Mixolydian Mode

A simple way to find the Mixolydian mode is to play any major scale and lower the seventh note scale by one half step (one fret).

A Mixolydian

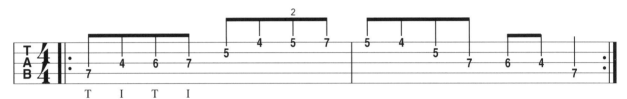

Here's another A Mixolydian scale.

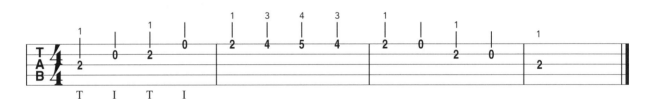

Modal Tip

You can also describe the Mixolydian mode as any major scale starting on its fifth note. If you play a D scale (D–E–F♯–G–A–B–C♯) starting on its fifth note, A, you're playing A Mixolydian (A–B–C♯–D–E–F♯–G). How elegant.

"Red Haired Boy" belongs to the reel family of tunes. It's also sometimes called "The Little Beggar Man." It is in the Mixolydian mode, and it's a real tune, indeed.

Track 69

Red Haired Boy

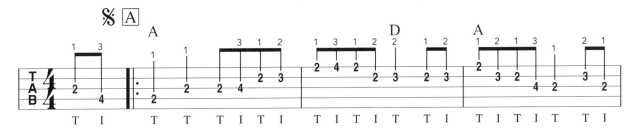

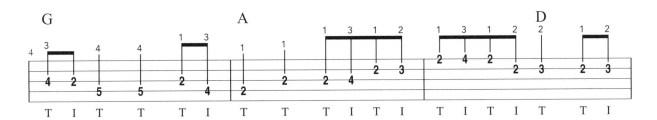

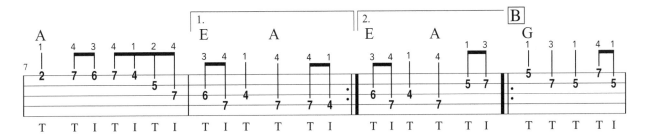

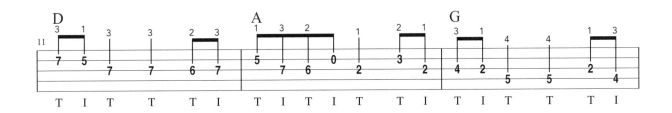

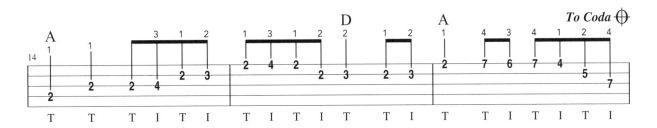

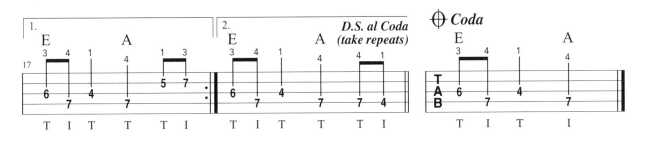

Harmony

Many books have been written on this subject. Webster's Dictionary offers a simple definition: "A musical agreement of sounds." The banjo is commonly tuned to a G chord. When you strum all of the strings, they are ringing in harmony with each other. A melody can be harmonized by playing along with different notes from the song's scale. This is what background singers often do. It is common to play a harmony part by starting on the note that is three scale steps higher from each melody note. Doing this is called "harmonizing in 3rds." Each harmony note is either a *major 3rd* (two whole steps above the melody note) or a *minor 3rd* (1 1/2 steps up).

After you learn this, play along with the CD. You are now harmonizing!

Track 71

Red Haired Boy
(Melody Played up a 3rd)

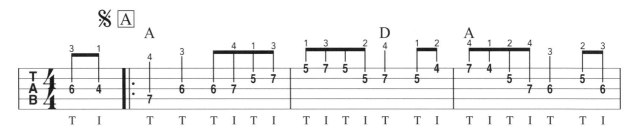

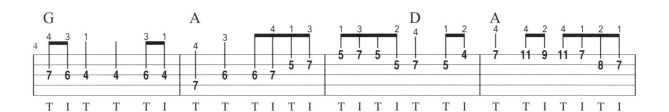

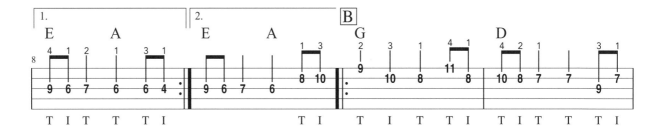

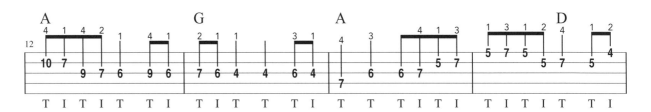

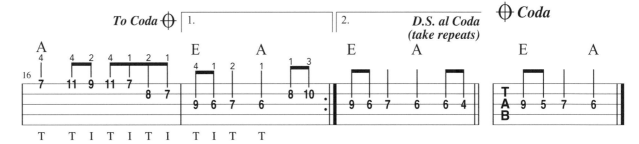

More Single-String Scales

The D scale below is associated with the D chord shape. These are all scale tones; the D shape is shaded for you to see. Play it ascending and descending.

Here it is in tab:

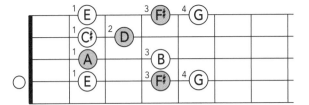

This next scale lies in front of the D shape. Visualize it as playing up to the A (or barre) shape D chord at the 7th fret (shaded area). This starts on the third note of the D scale (F♯), but now you play that note with the first finger of your left hand.

Here it is in tab:

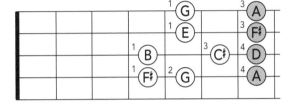

The Silver Spear High Break Ideas

After familiarizing yourself with D scales (and their associated chord shapes), play them up an octave. Start by finding the D-shape D chord above the 12th fret. Play the scale through the chord just as you did in the lower position, then play the second scale up to the next D chord, the A shape, at the 19th fret. This is the region where lies our next tune, "The Silver Spear."

The triplets played in "The Silver Spear" are treated as ornaments. They in themselves are not integral to the melody of the tune—they're icing on the cake. When used tastefully, ornaments provide variation. If they were used all the time in the same way, they would fail to provide contrast.

Some Ornament Alternatives

Repeat the excerpts below as written to get a fluent, easy feel so they can be used at your will and whimsy.

The first measure below works well in measures 1, 3, and 5.

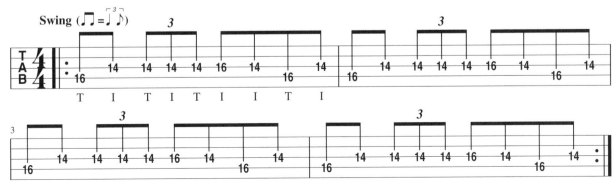

The triplet in measure 6 crosses strings. Here it is isolated for practice.

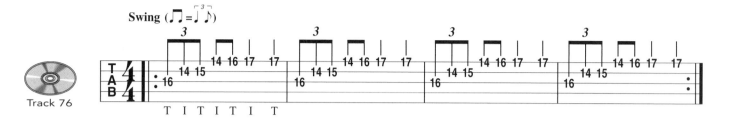

Track 76

Here's the same measure with no triplets.

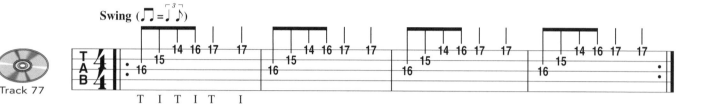

Track 77

T–I–M Triplets

Track 78

The following method allows you to play rapid-fire triplets with minimal effort. They are picked with the thumb, index, and middle fingers of the right hand (T–I–M).

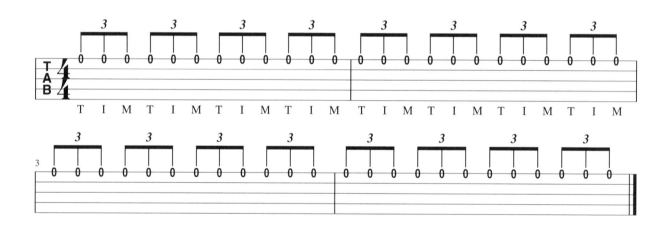

The triplets below fit well in measures 12 and 14.

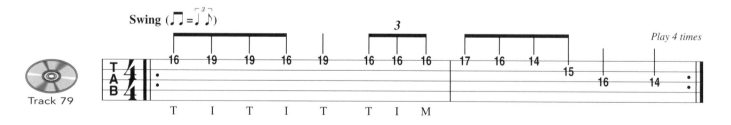

Track 79

The Silver Spear
(Single-String High Break)

Swing (♫ = ♩♪)

► Perhaps it'd be fun for you to explore playing this high break an octave lower.

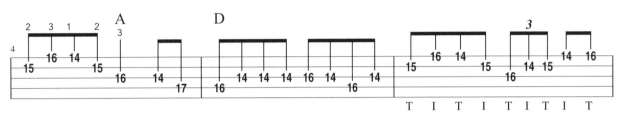

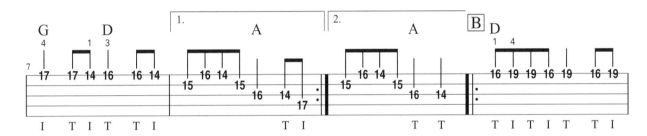

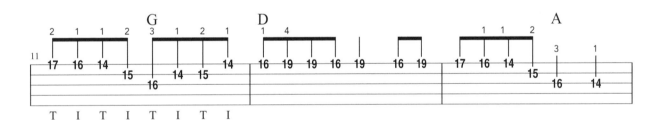

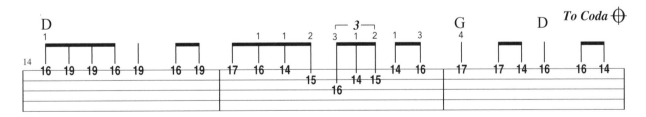

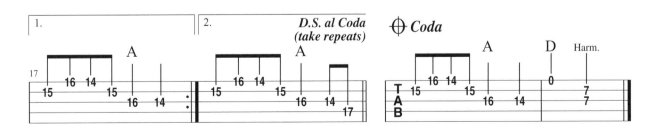

Track 81

Single-String Style in 6/8
Switching Fingers

When playing single-string triplets, you'll notice that the first group of three notes starts with the right-hand thumb, while the second group starts with the index finger.

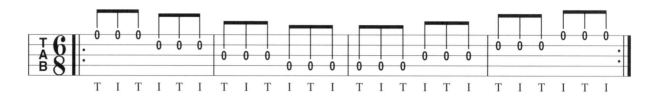

Track 82

D Major Scale—Open Position

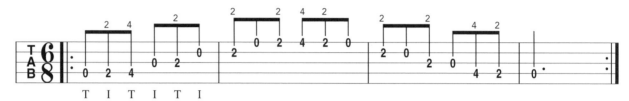

Track 83

D Mixolydian

We can play D Mixolydian by flatting the seventh note of the D major scale.

► D Mixolydian is the same as starting the G major scale on its fifth note, D.

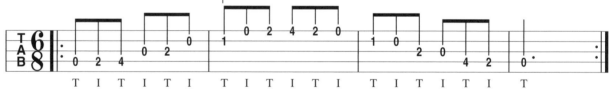

"Banish Misfortune?" Sounds like a good idea. Learning this three-part jig in D Mixolydian is surely a good start.

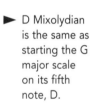

Track 84

Banish Misfortune

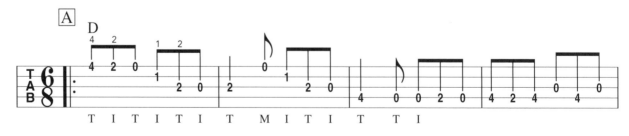

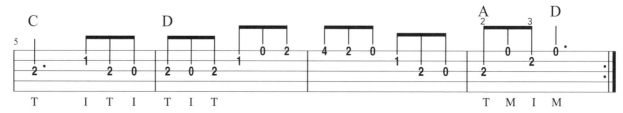

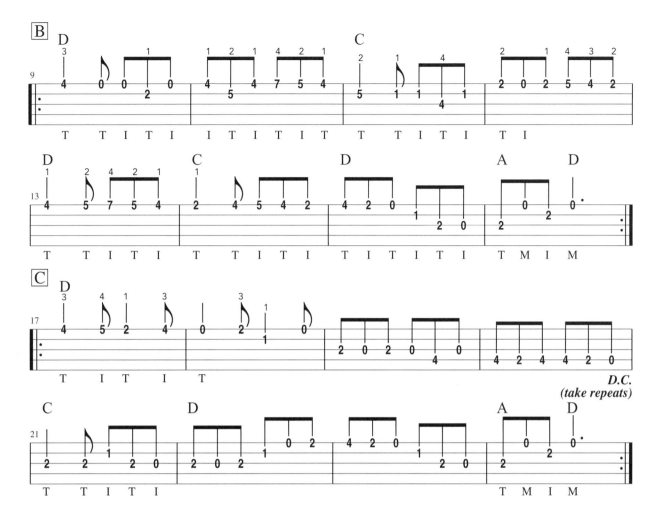

Banish Misfortune Ornament Alternatives

When you play notes in a series of half steps (no fret in between), it is called *chromatic*.

Measures 8 and 16 are nice places for this little chromatic run.

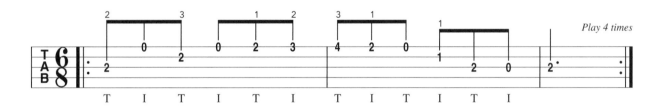

Here's a hammer-on/pull-off ornament that sounds nice in measure 15.

Here's another place for an ornament in measure 17.

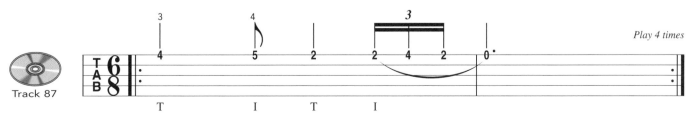

Track 88

The Road to Lisdoonvarna
(High Break)

The pull-off in measure 3 could also be picked with the index finger instead.

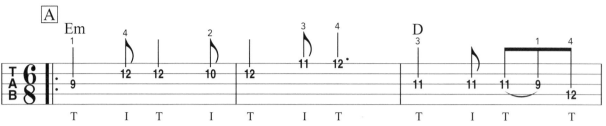

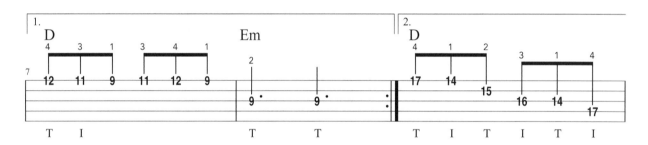

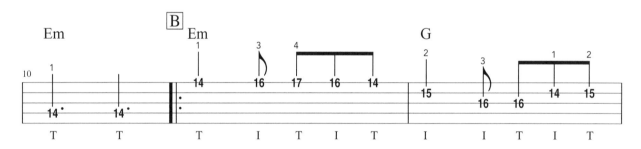

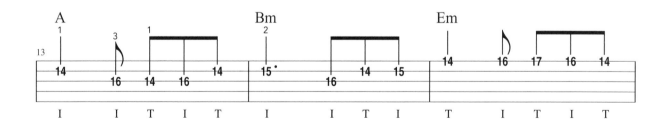

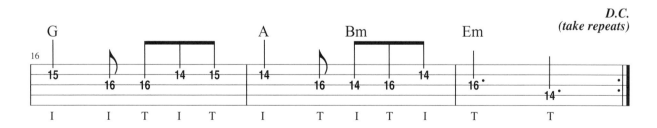

40

Lesson 11 | Combining Styles

Track 89

Track 90

The contrasting sound of the single-string and melodic styles can work together in the same piece. Here are four pieces that use both styles.

Red Haired Boy

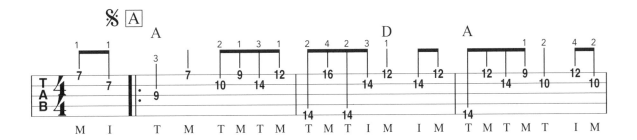

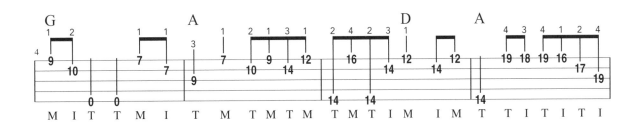

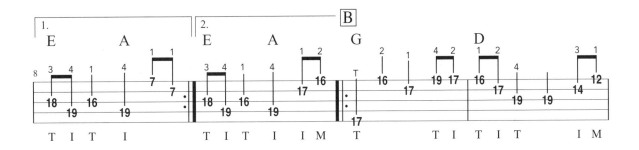

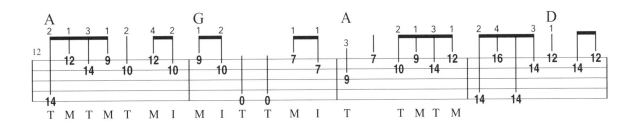

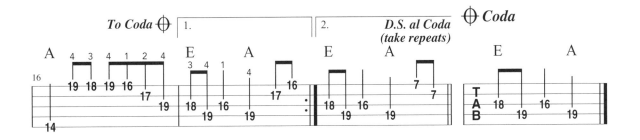

The Mason's Apron

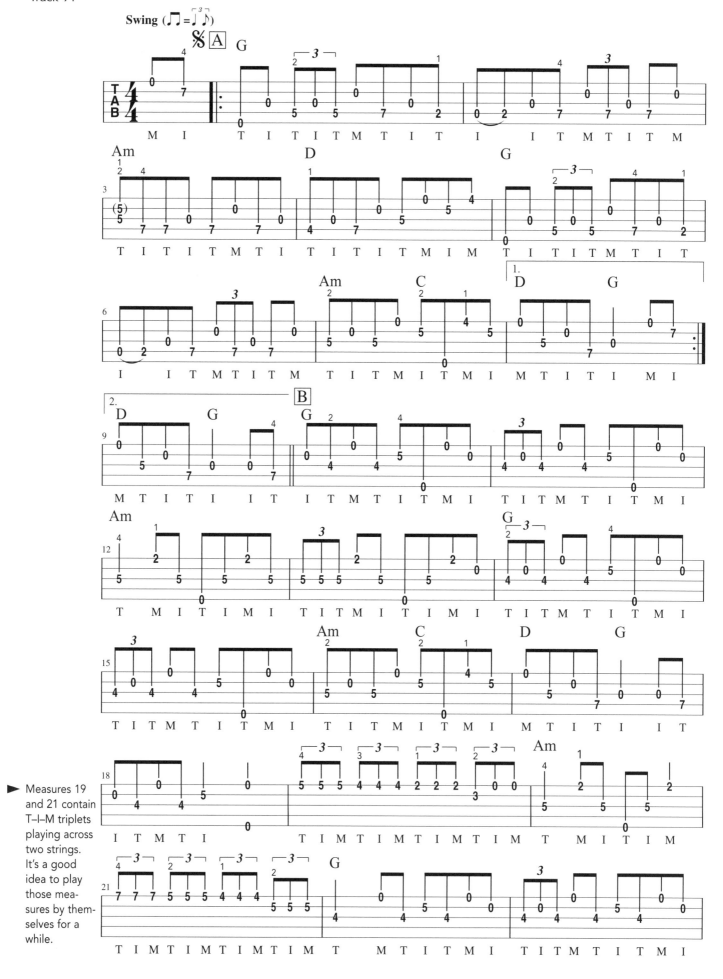

Measures 19 and 21 contain T–I–M triplets playing across two strings. It's a good idea to play those measures by themselves for a while.

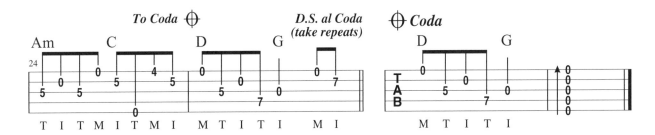

Track 92

Fisher's Hornpipe

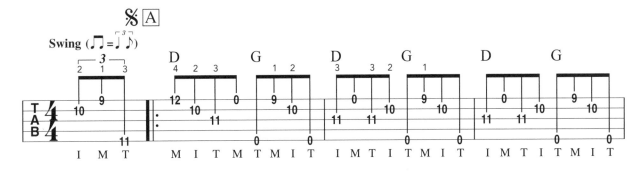

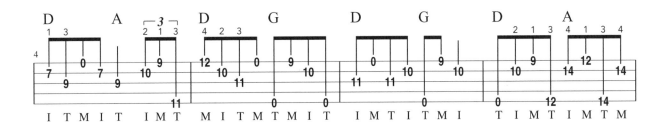

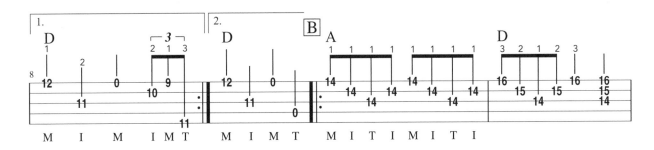

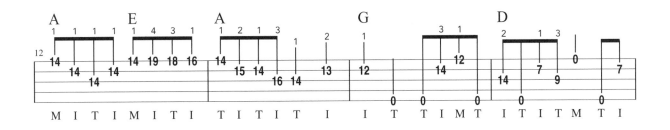

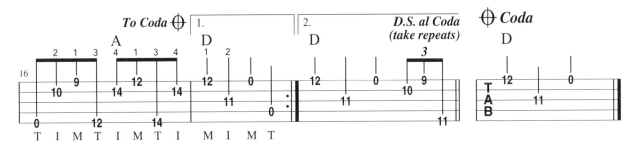

Morrison's Jig

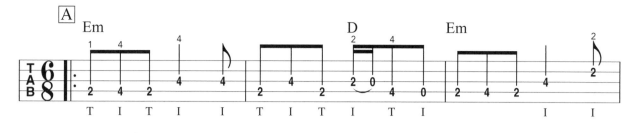

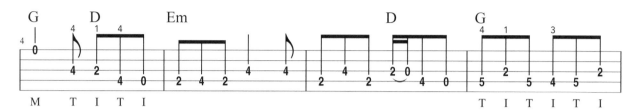

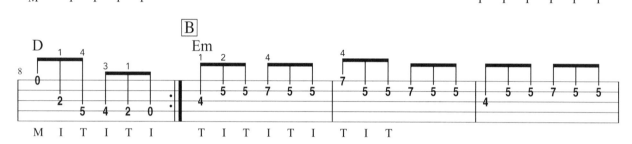

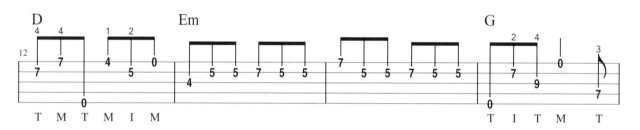

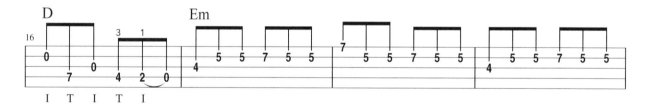

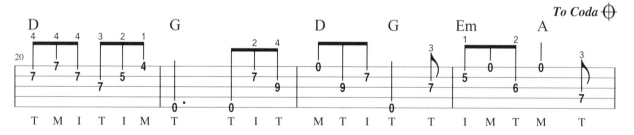

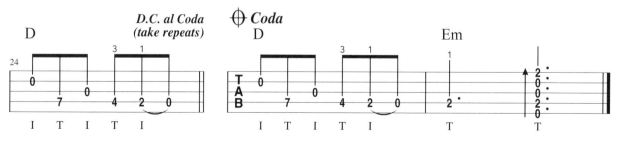

Chord Melody

Track 94

All the pieces in this book (and just about everywhere else) have melodies and chords. In music it's common to have someone play the chords (backup) while another player takes the melody or solo. In a chord melody arrangement, however, you play both the chords and the melody at the same time! Much has been written about chord melody for jazz guitar. The art of playing and arranging in this style has much to do with selecting a chord that sounds right with the melody while selecting notes from the chord that both imply its quality (major, minor, etc.) and support the melody. Common notes used are the root, 3rd, 5th, 6th, and 7th notes of the given chord. Conveniently, you need not (and could not) play the entire chord—just your well-selected notes from it. The chord melody approach gives the music a full sound and enables the banjoist to play unaccompanied. An entire book could be written on this subject!

Track 95

Auld Lang Syne

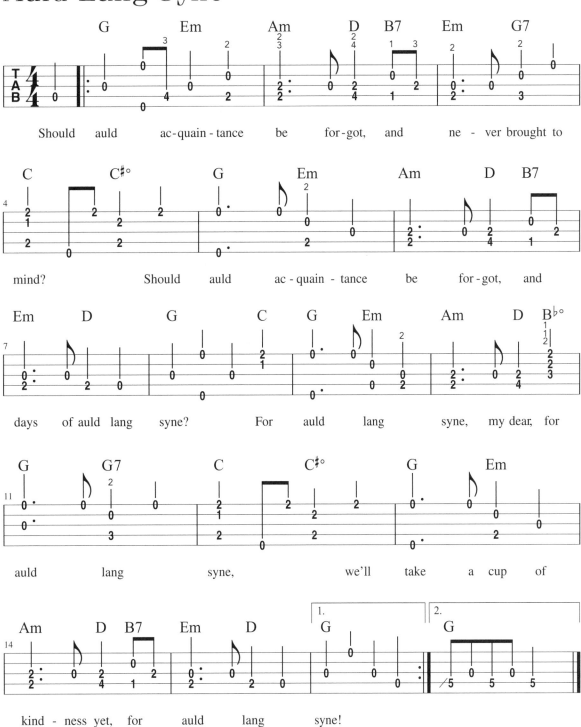

America the Beautiful

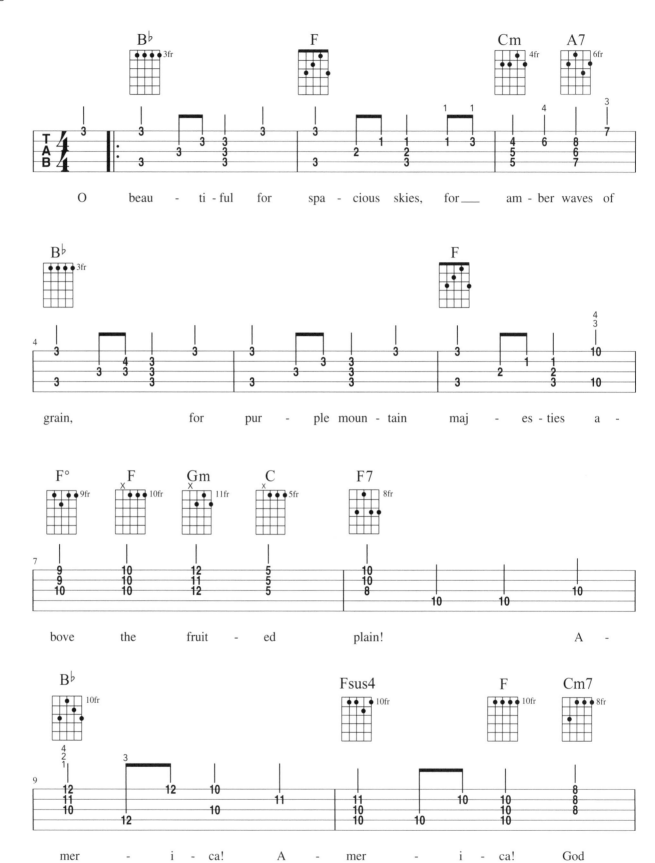

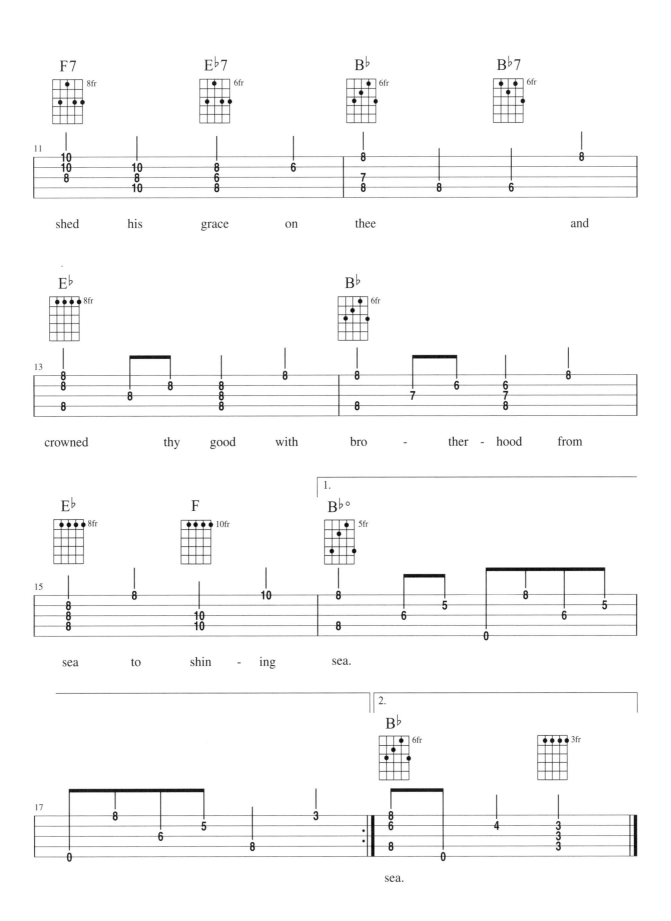

GREAT BANJO PUBLICATIONS
FROM HAL LEONARD CORPORATION